I See Greater

Seeing Beyond Life's Limitations

Jason L. Brownlee

Table of Contents

Introduction 1

Seventeen and Knowing 3

Walk It Out 11

I Can't Go Back. 23

The Snare is Broken 33

All By Faith 41

Faith to Forgive. 57

Overcoming the Fear of Failure .65

Fatherhood 73

Introduction

This nonfiction book is about a young man named Jason, who through faith and God's grace was able to see and excel beyond life's challenges and changes. Growing up in South Florida and moving to the Washington DC area, Jason's journey is filled with true testimonies and biblical references. It is an understatement to say that Jason's faith has transformed not only his life but the lives of those both far and near with a sense of humor and a heart for people. This book will inspire you to grow, go, and see greater.

Seventeen and Knowing

As a child growing up in South Florida my parents always said that there was something different about me from all the other children. I was the middle child of three sons, so I guess it wouldn't be hard to point out something peculiar about one of your children. After all, we ate from the same pots, drank from the same cups, and slept in the same house. So I often wondered what made me different.

I would frequently ask my parents questions like "Why am I here?" and "Is there really a tomorrow?" or "Will God do it today?" No matter what answer they gave me, it just wouldn't satisfy my curiosity. As a kid I can recall going to church all day on Sundays, singing in the choir, playing on the instruments, and listening to the preacher pour out from his soul. However, I seemed to be the only one after church with a different interpretation of the four hours and thirty-minute divine encounter that we all had just experienced. After Sunday dinner you could find me on the front porch singing, shouting, preaching, and praying, doing my very best to convey to anyone who cared to listen the way I experienced church that Sunday. I would reenact church and my brothers would just shake their heads while voicing to me, "This is way too much" and "That didn't happen." I would respond, "But this is the way that I see it." During my Sunday afternoon front porch revivals everybody got healed, saved, and delivered. No one had need of anything, the church roof wasn't leaking, and the air conditioner kept everyone nice and cool and to top it off, after church nobody had car trouble. My parents would attest years later that this wasn't just another child in the imagination stage of life. What was taking place in my heart was not just limited to our front porch or the four walls of our little church near the railroad tracks. The spirit of the Lord would come upon me on the walk to and from school and I would see everything with the possibility of being greater. These images of greater that I would see weren't just limited to myself or my immediate family. I would see a homeless man and visualize him in a mansion. I would see people struggling with sicknesses and picture them enjoying a healthy life. I would look at the most unfortunate circumstance and see total success. However, my report card from school seemed to be more challenging to see greater than I could ever imagine.

Often God would allow me to see visions and have dreams that I now understand were only previews of His glory that would be manifested in my life.

It was the summer of 1984 and by this time my mom and dad had decided that getting divorced would not stop them from being good parents, so with tear-filled eyes we watched my dad say goodbye. As you can only imagine, without my dad in the house my brothers and I got away with a lot more than the law allowed. My mother would work extra shifts at the local hospital to ensure that we had everything we needed.

By the time the summer of 1986 had ended and we were preparing for the start of another school year, my mother resolved that to bring in extra cash to provide for three sons who ate like an army, she would rent out a room in the house to a boarder. I can remember like it was yesterday: This short man with the tallest afro this side of heaven walking up to the door, ringing the bell and introducing himself as prophet, pastor, teacher, evangelist, reverend Dr. Marshall, and then started asking about the room that was for rent. I just stood there wondering, *This man is a prophet, pastor, teacher, evangelist, reverend, and doctor? So how many different people is this man inquiring about moving into our house, and are we going to receive rent from all of them?* My mother asked him a few questions before offering to show him the room and he responded, "I don't need to see the room; the Lord sent me." The short man with the big afro and the multiple titles moved in that same day.

My mother instructed my two brothers and me to refer to our new boarder as Prophet Marshall; nevertheless, behind closed doors I would just call him Shorty. You see, he may have gotten my mother's approval; however, my brothers and I still had some investigative work to do. I would watch Shorty like a hawk. I knew his comings and goings like the back of my hand. One night I got out of bed to go to the kitchen to get a late-night snack and as I walked by his room, I heard Shorty praying in a language that arrested my attention. I aborted my mission for a late-night snack and stood there it seemed like for hours just listening to this unknown language of prayer. That night I knew that there was something out of the ordinary about this Prophet Marshall. I would sit by the door of his room many nights just listening to him pray for hours on end.

As a youngster, being mischievous at times—perhaps more times than not—I often went looking for what God had not yet revealed and one day my two brothers and I did the unthinkable. It was one afternoon when no one was home that I shared with my brothers the strange things that had been going on with Shorty. They just stood in utter disbelief, laughing hysterically, as I did my best to imitate Shorty's prayer language. After they stopped laughing and pulled themselves together, I convinced them that we should enter Shorty's room and look around to see what he was really about. My directions to my brothers were not to touch or move anything. We formed a plan and positioned my younger brother outside the room as a lookout, and my older brother and I would do the dirty work and see who this prophet, pastor, teacher, evangelist, reverend Dr. Marshall really was. As we entered, the first thing that we noticed was that he didn't have a lot of things—just religious books, family pictures, and plenty of Kentucky Fried Chicken coupons. I broke my own rule and picked up a few of the prophet's books and read a couple of sentences and looked at some of his family pictures, making sure to leave nothing out of place. My brother pointed out to me some oil in a bottle on the side table and a pillow on the floor in front of the chair near the window. We exited Shorty's room with no indication that we had ever entered.

About three hours later Shorty arrived home. My brothers and I were in the front yard throwing the football, and before entering the house Shorty stopped and looked at me and my brothers and started laughing. Not knowing what to think, we stood there and watched as he laughed uncontrollably. Then Shorty looked right at me and said, "Your impression of my prayer language is one of the funniest things that I've ever heard or seen." He went on to say, "The pictures that you were looking at are of my wife and children, who you will one day meet." He then said, "I have a gift for you" and went into his room, returned, and gave me the very books that I had picked up to read from. While looking at my brother, who had accompanied me into the room, Shorty began to explain that often God will lead him to pray in various directions, often toward the east, and that was the reason for the pillow on the floor near the chair by the window. Shorty began to educate us concerning the anointing oil on the table. Shorty then looked at me and said, "By the time that you are seventeen you will leave this place and there will be a great change in your life." He went on to say, "You will preach the gospel of Jesus Christ." He declared again, "By the time you're seventeen you will know without a doubt that the hand of God is upon your life and God has given you the gift of faith, and this gift of faith will enable you to see greater, do greater, and become greater." With authority and power, he spoke these words unto me: "Now therefore stand and see this great thing, which the LORD will do before your eyes." Afterwards he reached into his bag and handed me and my brothers three coupons and a bucket of Kentucky Fried Chicken. That was life-changing; however, everyone knew that we were raised on Popeye's chicken and biscuits. I guess God didn't reveal that to the prophet, pastor, teacher, evangelist, reverend doctor, aka Shorty.

Not many days after that, Prophet Marshall announced that he would be moving out. I asked if it had anything to do with us violating his privacy. He smiled while shaking his head and said, "Not at all." He said that his assignment was up. I then understood that perhaps I was the assignment. God sent this prophet to ignite and expose me to the great things that God was going to do in me, through me, around me, and for me. This was just one of the divine encounters that God allowed me to experience that changed my life for the greater. Greater is what God has ordained for your life. I embraced that reality from that very day and refuse to settle for anything less.

Although life may not be easy, and the road often seems uphill, stay determined, greater is on the way. It's this mindset that won't allow you to sit in defeat. It's this mindset of greater that won't allow you to constantly complain about what's not happening for you yet. The Bible says it best in Proverbs 23:7: "For as he thinketh in his heart so is he." I challenge you to think greater than you've have ever thought before, and soon you'll begin to see what you've been saying.

One of my greatest joys on this journey of life is when God allows me to see greater for others. Sometimes I may not know a person's name or what they are facing in life but the same God that allowed Shorty to see and speak greater over my life will grace me to see and speak greater over the life of someone else. As you read this book or listen to this audio, I pray that you begin to see greater and speak greater, because the plans that God has for you are greater!

Walk It Out

Who Said You Couldn't Go There?

Joshua 1:3 (KJV)
³ Every place that the sole of your foot shall tread upon, that have I given unto you…

Seven to three, three to eleven, and eleven to seven. I remember these numbers quite well because they were scheduled shifts that my beloved mother would work to pay bills, meet the rent, and, as they would say in the urban community, make ends meet. Making ends meet seemed to be on the top of Mama's agenda every week. Mama worked at the local hospital as a unit secretary. Mama would tell my brothers and me that she liked working at the hospital because they allowed what was called floating. Floating was a terminology used to describe the altering of the monthly work schedule and shift changing. Every month I would witness Mama praying over that work schedule like Jesus in the Garden of Gethsemane, believing God would grant her favor to get the shift that would best allow her to pay bills, meet the rent, and make ends meet. We were raised to believe wholeheartedly in prayer and faith, but I think it's safe to say that Mama had an inside connection that would help God by leaking the upcoming monthly schedule to her. This would give Mama a jump on who would be on and who requested off and with that inside information, and every one of her coworkers' phone numbers memorized, Mama would get on the phone with that divulged monthly work schedule in one hand, and three multi-colored highlighters in the other hand, and walk between the kitchen, dining room, and living room on the telephone, convincing her coworkers that she would cover their shifts for overtime or just to give them an added day off on the monthly work schedule. Mama would then highlight it on her calendar as a reminder that she had committed herself to work seven to three, three to eleven, or eleven to seven. It was amazing to see Mama work that schedule like a bookie on fight night in Vegas. I could watch Mama's walk and tell when things were working out on the schedule the way she wanted. Understand, Mama's walk would tell it all. She would go from a kitchen stroll to a dining room stride to a living room glide that said that she owned that schedule and was going to get whatever shift was necessary to pay bills, meet the rent, and make ends meet.

When I was fourteen years old, we moved from our small suburban home in Deerfield Beach, Florida, about fifteen miles south to the city of Ft. Lauderdale. We relocated to a part of the city called Lauderhill. On this side of town one road divided two classes of people. On the one side of the highway was the projects, or at that time they were known as low-income housing, and on the other side there was a gated community for the well-to-do, with a secure checkpoint and a massive waterfall adorned with florescent lighting for the enjoyment of those waiting to be cleared to enter. This place was then known as the all-inclusive Inverrary resident and vacation resort. Some of the who's who of Ft. Lauderdale's elite A-listers were said to have taken up residence beyond those heavenly gates. Sometimes I would walk to the top of the street just to look over to see the people who lived the life of luxury as they entered and exited the all-inclusive Inverrary resident and vacation resort, and for some peculiar reason I just felt that I belonged over there among them. There would be all classes of expensive cars: Rolls Royce, Mercedes Benz, and limousines lined up waiting to gain access beyond those heavenly gates. I would stand and stare in awe and astonishment, imagining what it would be like to have the experience of going beyond those gates.

I can recall like it was yesterday: It was on one of south Florida's many hot summer days that Mama had worked one of her floating shifts. Mama returned home and beckoned me with a list for dinner to walk to the local grocery store that sat adjacent to the entrance of the all-inclusive Inverrary resident and vacation resort. Before handing me the list Mama said to me, "Jason, go to the store and come right back." This wasn't good because I had already planned it out; you see, if I ran to the store I would reserve a few minutes to watch the cars entering and exiting the all-inclusive Inverrary resident and vacation resort. However, every time I thought that I was being released, Mama would retract the grocery list, either to add or subtract something that she had forgotten or didn't need to stay within budget. Finally, I had my updated, modified, and multi-edited, completely approved grocery list. Just as I was on the way out the door with my revised grocery itinerary clenched in my fist, Mama said the seven deadly words that would kill the joy of my side mission: "Wait, I'm going to go with you." I almost burst into tears.

Please understand whenever Mama went to the store, that grocery list went out the window. Mama only purchased what she had expiring coupons for or what was on sale. This meant we purchased more than we ever intended and again I would have to use my unauthorized authority to extend the shopping cart restricted areas to reach beyond the parking lot just to get the groceries home.

While walking with Mama to the local grocery store that sat adjacent to the entrance of the all-inclusive Inverrary resident and vacation resort, I asked, "Why can't we go over there?" Mama looked deep in my eyes and replied, "Who told you that we couldn't go over there?" Before I could answer, Mama had taken me by the hand and was walking me across the street toward the gates of the all-inclusive Inverrary resident and vacation resort. I began to take notice that the closer we got to the gate, the more Mama's walk changed. She went from a project stroll to a middle class stride to an all-inclusive Inverrary resident and vacation resort glide, and there we were walking through the very gates of the place that so many were waiting to gain access to. How could this be? No one asked us anything. We changed our walk and entered right in.

It was that day that I understood that a person's walk reflects their mood, emotions, and personality. Believe it or not, people are watching the way you walk; it tells them something about you. How you walk is an indication to the world around you that either you own or don't belong. My mama looked me in the eyes and said, "Jason, don't ever let anyone tell you what you can't have or where you can or can't go in life. Just change your walk and go possess it. After all, isn't that what God told Joshua? 'Every place that the sole of your foot shall tread upon, that have I given unto to you.'"

I've learned that the foot has three major parts: the toe, the heel, and the sole. The toe is the part of the foot that represents momentary stability. Unless your name is Michael Jackson, you can't stand on your toes that long. The heel is the part of the foot of uncertainty. Many of us have been pushed back on the heels of uncertainty but thanks be to God, there's a part of the foot called the sole. The sole is the part of the foot the represents confidence. So while you're walking toward your destiny, walk with confidence, walk with certainty, walk with conviction that says you also belong in the all-inclusive Inverrary resident and vacation resort.

I've learned that the greatest way to walk is by faith. It's the faith walk that walks us out of the brokenness and bondage that's holding us back. It's the faith walk that's walking us through and into the destiny that God has ordained for our lives. Walking by faith says even when you don't see the staircase, you still take steps. Remember, it's not the size of your steps that's most important but that you keep taking steps. Walking implies steady movement. Movement is a mandate for anyone who's destined to lead and make a difference. I've witnessed the decision to make a move take lives from rags to riches, from good to greater, from better to best, and from obscurity to notoriety. In 2nd Kings chapter 7 it was a mindset to move that took four leprous men during a severe famine from poverty to prosperity.

These four men were sitting and deliberating with each other what to do when they asked themselves a question: "Why sit we here until we die?" It was at that moment they decided to get up and make a move. The story goes on to tell that as these four men were moving toward the city things were miraculously being moved out of the way. It's clear to see that when we consistently walk or move toward our desired objectives, God will divinely order oppositions to move out of our way. As we move God moves for us, around us, through us, and in us. The manifestation of the miracle is in the movement.

In Daniel chapter 3, three young Hebrew men stood up to a crazy, narcissistic king named Nebuchadnezzar. Because they refused to compromise these young men were thrown into a burning furnace that was heated seven times hotter. These young men decided that they wouldn't just lie down and die, but scriptures say they started walking while in the fire. While they were walking in the fire, king Nebuchadnezzar realized that Jesus was with them. The Bible goes on to tell that when they came out of the furnace, they didn't even smell like smoke. Walking it out has a way of getting us through it and then getting it off us.

I am sure that there are many with the same testimony that you had to keep walking. As a pastor I speak all the time with people who made the choice to keep walking. Despite going through unimaginable circumstances, they kept walking, some through sickness, others through shame, some through the loss of a loved one, and others through unforeseen misfortune. They all have the same testimony, we had to keep it moving.

When Mama and I exited the grocery store I could hear the store manager in the distance screaming, "The shopping carts are restricted to the parking lot," again and again screaming at the top of his voice, "The shopping carts are restricted to the parking lot." Mama said to me in a small, firm voice, "Baby, keep walking." I'm not endorsing heisting shopping carts from local grocery store parking lots. I'm saying walk until every negative voice is drowned in the distance. Keep walking, no matter what life presents; keep walking and you'll see that every restraint and restriction will become a distant memory and a voice of the past.

There was a great wall that stood between Israel and the entering of the Promised Land. God gave clear instructions to Joshua for the army of Israel to do one thing: walk around the walls. Joshua commanded the army to walk around the wall for seven days in formation. Their walk was an open demonstration of their forward momentum and fearless faith. If there's anything I know firsthand, it's fearless faith will keep you walking. I'm convinced that lasting success is not a mad dash to the finish line but a walk of formation, forward momentum, and fearless faith. After Israel walked around the walls for seven days, the walls fell flat, and Israel took the city. The key to this great victory was no matter how it looked, they kept walking.

This reminds me of the story of two frogs down on the farm jumping from log to log. One day they both fell into a bucket of milk. One frog looked at the other and said how wonderful it had been jumping from log to log on sunny days and rain-filled afternoons, but he was convinced that it was now over. It was at that moment that he gave up and sank to the bottom of the bucket. The other frog thought about all the wonderful things he wanted to accomplish, the vacations he had planned to enjoy, the business ventures that he had yet to attempt. He thought about his family and friends that he wanted more time to enjoy. It was at that moment that he decided that he would keep moving, and the milk turned into butter, and he walked out of that bucket. It doesn't matter what your bucket may be; just keep walking and things will turn around for your benefit and you will walk out of it. Make up your mind to keep moving.

In 2020 I was affected like so many with the Covid-19 virus. As you can imagine, this was a very uncertain time in my life, to say the least. Watching the news and listening to the radio, it was clear that the world was in an unprecedented panic. It was this panic that paralyzed our comings and goings from what we once knew. We were shut up in our homes with little to no mobility. While I was watching television one afternoon, a commercial came on that said, "A body in motion stays in motion." After being told that I was Covid positive and feeling the worst that I'd ever felt in my life, I knew that if I was going to get through this, I had to keep moving. I lay seven days in a hospital and after day two, I knew that I needed to get up and start walking. The nurse would come into the room and tell me to get back in the bed. I would respond, "I've got to walk this out."

I want to pause and say, God bless all those physicians, nurses, and hospital staff that not only had to walk through this pandemic but carried the weight of caring for so many who were hospitalized by this. I'm forever grateful. While lying in the hospital I began to think on the scripture that says, in Psalms 23:4 (KJV), "Yea, though I walk through the valley of the shadow of death, I will fear no evil." I truly believe making up my mind to keep walking got me through it.

It's been a few years since that frightful experience, but I'm determined to encourage as many people as possible to keep moving. Many will agree that life will present countless challenges, but every challenge can be overcome if we can just keep moving. Just as the milk turned to butter because that frog refused to stop moving, I'm a witness that if you can refuse to give up and just keep moving, it's only a matter of time before things turn in your favor and you walk out, walk over, and walk through whatever challenges you will ever face. My doctor once said to me that walking was the best form of exercise. I asked, "Don't you mean that running is the best form of exercise?" He smiled and said, "You can walk a lot farther than you can run." As I thought about it, I had to admit that he was right: A good walk can last a lot longer than a run. So if business is going to prosper, one must be willing to take the walk; if ministry is going to last, be willing to take the walk; if marriage is going to work, be willing to take the walk.

I've learned over time that it's not always about how fast we arrive at our destinations but the wisdom and revelation we gain over the course of the journey. In Genesis chapter 32 (KJV) there was a man named Jacob who was left alone, and while in that place of isolation the Bible says that Jacob wrestled with a man until the breaking of the day. Anybody who knows anything about wrestling knows that it's a combination of pulling and applying pressure, for the purpose of pinning your opponent down. As they pulled, applied pressure, and attempted to pin one another down, the Bible says that Jacob was the more dominant. The man touched the hollow of Jacob's thigh and Jacob's thigh was out of joint as he wrestled. It was at that moment that the man told Jacob to let him go, but Jacob replied, "Not until you have blessed me." The man replied, "Let me go, for the day breaks." Jacob again responded, "I won't let you go until you bless me." Jacob was determined that he was not going to leave that place of pressure and pulling the same way.

The Bible tells us that Jacob was blessed, and his life was preserved. However, Jacob walked away from that place with a limp. It is safe to say that there is a depth of determination, willpower, and resolve to be better that will sometimes cause you to walk away with a limp. I have a newfound respect for people I see who walk with any level of difficulty, knowing that life may have tried to pressure, pull, or pin them but they were determined to win.

I once met a Vietnam vet who walked on prosthetics. He shared with me what he and many other soldiers had experienced in the war. He ended his story with these words: "I refused to give up and was determined to walk again." I've had the opportunity to talk with many who walked with physical limps, some with emotional limps, while others have had to endure financial limps, or relational limps, but they all have this in common: They all were determined to walk again. If there's anything that I've learned in life, it is the win in life is not always how fast you arrive but that you're determined to keep moving.

I Can't Go Back

Totally Committed

1ˢᵗ Kings 19:20 (KJV)
²⁰ *And he left the oxen, and ran after Elijah, and said,*
Let me, I pray thee, kiss my father and my mother,
and then I will follow thee. And he said unto him,
Go back again: for what have I done to thee?

It was the summer of 1989, and the day was July 4th. Two days earlier I received the phone call that would change my life forever. I was only seventeen when my dad called and asked if my two brothers and I would like to travel with him to Washington, DC for about two weeks for a job-related event. I couldn't believe it; just a month before I received this call I was in school sitting in my social studies class when I noticed someone had left a book under my desk with a picture of the nation's capital on the back of it. I leaned over to the person next to me and said, "Washington, DC the place of movers and shakers—that's where I'm going," and less than one month later, while everyone in "Peril City," the low income housing project we lived in, was making plans to celebrate the Fourth of July I was packing what little belongings I owned. All I could think about the night before was that my two brothers and I were about to take the trip to The Chocolate City, aka Washington, DC. It was about 5 a.m. when my dad arrived to pick us up. Needless to say, I was up, packed and ready go. My dad noticed that I had somehow packed everything that had some kind of significance to me. My dad looked at me and said in a very authoritative voice that we couldn't bring anything but a few changes of clothes and a bag lunch. While my two brothers—under their breath, of course—expressed their disappointment at our dad's packing instructions, I was willing to leave it all behind in preparation to go forward. I really can't explain it, but it was as if I knew that I wasn't coming back.

We departed early the next morning before the sun began to rise and for some strange reason, I could feel it in my innermost being that this would be my last ride as a resident through the streets of Peril City housing projects. While we were departing, I can remember saying to myself, *Don't look back because you can't go back.* We continued through the side streets to make our way to the main highway and then onto Interstate 95 North. That's when it hit me: everything that life had for me was ahead of me, and not behind me. I just kept saying to myself, *I can't go back.* The truth of the matter is I didn't know what to expect moving forward, but I knew it felt better than the feeling of being stuck. From the time my parents divorced until moving to Washington, DC, I felt that I was in a cycle of just being stuck. Moving from place to place and yet still stuck. Believing that life had more to offer but yet still stuck. I know I'm not the only one with this testimony that life has so much more to offer but you just feel stuck, sometimes praying that some great fortune would happen to help you get free. Well, I guess God heard my prayers and sent the most unlikely way out that I could have ever imagined.

Please understand I really believe that my dad meant well with what he said, but his definition of "I'm on the way" could possibly mean "I'll see you in about thirty days if I still decide to come." Or "there was a change of plans, and I didn't feel the need to tell you anything." I quickly learned that "I'll be right back" could really mean "when I get back is when I'll be back." With this understanding of communication, you could image the uncertainty that I was feeling that night before my dad's arrival. However, even with this history of uncertainty of communication, I was fully certain that this was my answer to get unstuck.

When we arrived in Washington DC, I knew I was out of the projects and I wasn't ever going back. My first week in the big city, I soon noticed that people were far different than folk in the South. Growing up in South Florida, we created a culture that so many are yet proud of to this very day. Our music sounded different, and our urban dialect could only be understood if you grew up in the 305 area code. We looked up to guys who could take an old 64 Impala drop top or a 77 Chevy Nova and trick it out with a sound system that could be heard for at least five blocks, a paint job with more metal than Liberace had diamonds, and custom rims that were more expensive than the whole car itself. To top it off, we would wear our own style of clothes and hairstyles that shined brighter than the Southern sun. In my mind at that time, I was convinced that this was all life had to offer, but after one week in Washington, DC I was exposed to a world that I soon came to realize was bigger than the 305 area code we lived in.

Today my family and I often travel to Ft. Lauderdale for rest and relaxation, and it's hard to believe that this is the very place that I experienced so much happiness and hardship. Then one day it just settled upon me that prosperity and poverty begin and end with your mentality. I vowed never to go back to the mentality that kept us in poverty. Leaving the past behind is easier said than done. There are families who lived in the projects when I was a kid who are still living in the same projects to this very day. The reason is that many have a hard time letting go of the past or the present to reach for a greater future. Please understand that destiny requires making a decision. When I reflect, I now realize that I didn't choose Washington, DC. However, God allowed Washington, DC to choose me. Hear me when I say when Washington, DC chose me. I had to make a destiny decision. That destiny decision was to leave everything that I'd ever known behind. I mean everything. The culture I grew up knowing, the climate I grew up enjoying, and the kinfolk I grew up holding so dear to journey into the unknown. What a day that was, at the young age of seventeen and cutting ties to continue. Life is no different today. Many will come to the knowledge that to continue they must be willing to cut ties. That's right, cutting ties is sometimes necessary to step up, out, and into what life has for you.

I soon came to realize that going forward would require that I commit to not ever going back. It's that commitment that set the stage for a new life of success and victory. In all honesty, commitment is a word that many use but few live up to. Commitment is the very thing that makes the difference in living a life of victory or defeat. It's the transformation of releasing the past and reaching for the future.

Consider this: When Jesus called His disciples, He made it clear that without commitment they couldn't effectively follow Him. He said to them in St. Mark 8:34 (KJV), "Whosoever will come after me, let him deny himself and take up his cross and follow me." The moment that we make a commitment, it changes the direction of our lives. The true continuation of commitment entails the denial of self. This commitment demands total devotion. This magnitude of commitment is responsible for exposing countless individuals to a level of determination that rewards and grants the reality of living your dream.

Let's be clear: There are multiple levels of commitment, and I have discovered four stages that will impact your performance and productivity. I've encountered individuals in life for whom commitment wasn't a thought, let alone an action. They possessed an attitude that was very casual concerning commitment. This casual commitment can be seen in a manner of inconsistency and carelessness. It's a mindset of if I do, I do, and if I don't, I don't. Casual commitment is the result of many quitting before they start and giving up before they began. This is the reason some are always late and leave early and can never complete tasks and meet deadlines. Casual commitment yields no success and is the pathway to poverty and unproductiveness. The Bible says it best in Proverbs 10:4 (KJV): "He becometh poor that dealeth with a slack hand."

Another level of commitment is the communicative commitment. I can say with certainty that we all have seen or heard of someone with this level of commitment. They are the ones who articulate but take no action; they get excited about the opportunity but never do anything. They are always talking loud but ain't saying nothing. Proverbs 14:23 (NLT) says it best: "Work brings profit, but mere talk leads to poverty!"

There's another form of commitment that I call coerced commitment. That's the kind of commitment that waits for someone else to say that they'll go or do something before that individual decides to make a move. They have to constantly be coerced in order to commit to anything. They are more concerned about what others think or say than they are about what they think of themselves. They are often fearful and doubtful about what they're going to do and how they're going to go about it. They sit back to see what others are going to do before they make a move, then base their commitment upon someone else's allegiance. They say things like "I will if you will, but if you don't, I won't" and often they only do what the others do. They have to be pushed and persuaded to put forth any effort toward anything. In the book of Judges chapter four Barak wouldn't commit without Deborah, therefore she told him that he wouldn't receive the honor for the victory. How many times have so many missed out waiting on someone to coerce them to commit?

There's another form of commitment that I call clinging commitment. This kind of commitment guarantees success on every level. It's seen throughout history in those who have achieved greatness and left great legacies. It's this form of commitment that pleases God. This level of commitment is where many make their declaration of destiny decision. The Bible tells of the story of Jacob being left alone and wrestling with an angel. It's recorded that the angel caused Jacob's thigh to be out of joint while wrestling but he refused to give up and let go. Jacob declared, "I won't let you go except you bless me." What a level of commitment displayed by Jacob that regardless of the pain he still maintained his clinging commitment.

There's a woman in the Bible by the name of Ruth who had a clinging commitment far beyond any that I've ever seen or heard of. Her husband had died, and she was left in a famine with her sister-in-law Orpah and her mother-in-law Naomi. She made a clinging commitment that many would call crazy. Her mother-in-law gives it to Ruth and Orpah straight. Naomi tells her two daughters-in-law that her own husband is dead and her two sons are dead as well. She goes on to let them know that she has nothing left to promise them a prosperous future. Naomi then advises them to go on their way and seek a life somewhere that may seem promising. The Bible records that they began to cry and then Orpah kissed her mother-in-law farewell but Ruth clung to her with these words: "Intreat me not to leave thee, *or* to return from following after thee: for whither thou goest, I will go; and where thou lodgest, I will lodge: thy people *shall be* my people, and thy God my God. Where thou diest, will I die, and there will I be buried: the LORD do so to me, and more also, if ought but death part thee and me." Ruth clung to and committed to Naomi when she had nothing to offer and looked as if she was going nowhere.

True commitment is not about convenience. It's not about being comfortable. It's not about doing what seems easy at the moment. True commitment is not about you at all. True commitment is about the cause. If you can find a cause that's worthy of your commitment, it will birth a determination that sees beyond any barrier, bad news, or broken promises. Your cause will push you out of bed before the crack of dawn and keep you up to early morning hours. True commitment to a worthy cause will push you beyond your human limitation and then ask for more. You and I could name countless individuals who discovered causes worth their commitment and achieved great success. Your commitment to whatever and whoever will only be as great as the cause is to you.

Ruth saw Naomi as a cause worth committing to. Despite Naomi having nothing to offer, Ruth committed her whole life to what others would deem as unworthy. As a result of Ruth's unwavering commitment, she was blessed with a new life, a new love, and new a lineage.

I believe it's imperative that we understand the true components of commitment. Commitment is a matter of decision. Until you make the decision to commit, then at best, you'll just wander through life being tossed and driven by life's circumstances. Commitment is also a matter of direction. Clear direction gives us the certainty that we are in pursuit of a worthy cause. Commitment is a matter of denial. The greatest level of discipline is self-denial. Commitment is a matter of dying to self. Dying to self is the sacrifice that's essential for great success. Commitment is a matter of devotion. Devotion is the confirmation that you will continue to follow through on your commitment. God honors commitment and commitment honors God.

One of the greatest examples of commitment is when Elisha runs after Elijah. The prophet Elijah finds Elisha plowing behind twelve yoke of oxen. When Elisha sees Elijah and knows that his destiny is not in plowing behind oxen, he runs after Elijah with the intent to totally commit. He takes the oxen and the instruments and burns them, leaving himself no way back to that former life. In essence, what Elisha was saying was "I can't go back." Elisha was committed, no matter the journey. This journey of commitment took Elisha from a place called Gilgal, which is the place of a fresh start, to a place called Bethel, which is known as a place of God's presence, to Jericho, the place of testing, and to Jordan, the place of crossing over. It was commitment that kept Elisha connected to Elijah as they journeyed and came to the place of his destiny. It was commitment that caused him to receive a double portion of what was on the life of Elijah.

I'm convinced that commitment is essential to keep us moving forward with a mindset that *I can't go back*. Whatever God has graced you to come away from, I pray that you continue in the spirit that's determined to go forward and refuses to go back.

The Snare is Broken
Breaking the Barrier of Bigotry

Psalms 124:7 (KJV)
⁷ Our soul is escaped as a bird out of the snare of the fowlers: the snare is broken, and we are escaped.

I'm sure that many who grew up in the 60s, 70s, and 80s can attest to the racial ramifications that still resound to this very day. I can personally recall as a kid hearing where I could and couldn't go, what I could and couldn't have, who I could and couldn't become friends with. When I was fifteen years of age, I was repeatedly told by a racist teacher in high school that by the time I turned eighteen I would be in jail and probably wouldn't live to see my twenty-fifth birthday.

These asinine experiences of racism didn't leave me half as concerned as what I encountered in my own community. Growing up in the late seventies and eighties, I was forced to deal with the bigotry of the black community.

This prejudice was not predicated upon what kind of car you drove, what name brand clothes you wore, or what neighborhood you lived in. This discrimination in the black community was purely determined by the darkness of your skin and the texture of your hair. Can you imagine one of the very things that you couldn't change about yourself seemed to be a charge against you among people who had chosen to inflict the same racism that they were experiencing or once experienced? If you were a light-skinned black you were preferred and if you were a dark-skinned black you were pushed to the back and made to feel inferior. Not only did I sometimes have to face the injustice of my white counterparts, but it only added insult to injury to constantly feel this same injustice in my own community.

My most memorable experience of bigotry was when I was just in the second grade—yes, the second grade. I was seven years old, and I can remember my teacher who we will call Ms. Bias. She was a tall, thin, dark-skinned, kinky-haired black woman from a little town in the deep South called who the hell knows. At the beginning of this particular school day Ms. Bias made an announcement to the class. The announcement went like this: "All the students who are polite and behave themselves and complete their assignment will receive a pretzel at the end of the day." Hear me when I tell you, I wanted that pretzel and was willing to be the most well-mannered student in the world. I behaved myself better than any child in the history of human behavior and completed my assignments, along with any extra credit work that was recommended or required. Let me caution you that these were not just any pretzels, these were the much desired "you have to be polite, behave yourself, and complete your assignments by the end of the day" pretzels. Please understand that you couldn't buy this kind of pretzel. Ms. Bias expressed how proud of the class she was. Needless to say, our whole class was polite, everyone behaved themselves, and we all completed our assignments.

Then it happened: Ms. Bias began to hand out the pretzels. I noticed that she would skip over all the dark-skinned, kinky-haired children and give to only the light-skinned children. Not one of us dark-skinned children received a pretzel, and to make it worse, she sat in her seat and just watched us sit there while all those children who resembled El DeBarge, Gregory Abbot, and Al B. Sure ate their pretzels. I boldly got up from my seat with a determination that the Whoopi Goldbergs, Wesley Snipes, and Sidney Poitiers of our class were not going to be denied because of our deep, dark skin. So I walked to her desk and took my pretzel and began to hand pretzels to my other chocolate classmates.

At that moment Ms. Bias started screaming at me at the top of her voice to put the pretzels back and go sit down! I responded, "It's broken" with a conviction in my voice that arrested the attention of everyone on the hallway of our second-grade class. Again, I screamed, "It's broken." I was referring to the pretzel, but Ms. Bias knew that the only reason that she didn't give us pretzels was because she disliked herself and every time she looked at one of us dark-skinned babies she saw herself and it reminded her of the bigotry that she had come to believe in her own black community. Ms. Bias kept screaming until she caught the attention of another teacher across the hall, and I responded again, "It's broken," only referring to the pretzel that I was denied because of the darkness of my skin. However, I believe that God was using me to help free Ms. Bias from the biased behavior that held her back, kept her down, and pushed her aside.

Totally exhausted from trying to hold on to fragments of a pretzel and screaming repeatedly, I looked up and said in a voice just above a whisper, "Ms. Bias, it's broken." Ms. Bias responded with tear-filled eyes in a tone reflective of redemption, "Yes, it's broken." It was at that moment that the snare was broken, and we were free, never to be held back, kept down, or pushed aside by what others thought about our beautiful dark skin.

I write this because if we are not careful this seed of being made to feel inferior will begin to spout and flourish in other areas of life. I've counseled people who were overlooked, left out, and made to feel as if they just didn't belong. Often my advice is to try not to focus on what they think or say about you but more so what you think and say about yourself.

As I look back, I never allowed Ms. Bias' unpleasant perspective to change the view that was instilled in me before I ever crossed the threshold of her class. My daddy had a sister named Sadie. My aunt Sadie was the most fearless, confident, and respected woman I had ever come to know. Aunt Sadie would cut you a piece of her famous bread pudding and say, "You will never taste another piece of bread pudding this good as long as you live." My aunt Sadie would tell me that white folk wished they had the looks and style that God gave to us. She would tell me from the color of our skin to the texture of our hair, black people look more like Christ than any other people on the planet. Aunt Sadie told me, "Never forget that it's not what other folk think about you but what you think about yourself that makes the difference." She would say to me, "You are not the victim but you are the victorious." I think everybody needs an Aunt Sadie in their lives.

This is what the children of Israel lacked when they went to spy out the Promised Land. Numbers 13:33 (KJV): "...and we were in our own sight as grasshoppers, and so we were in their sight." They saw themselves as small and inadequate, so they assumed that they were seen as such. The truth is, you may encounter people who will attempt to make you feel less than or insufficient but remember, they are only showing you how they feel about themselves. Be sure not to fall into that snare. To see my daughter now as a teenager, adorned with natural hair and beautiful chocolate skin, conduct herself with a confidence that's certain of success causes me to understand that the snare is broken, and we have escaped.

I vowed to myself never to be entangled ever again with the depression of other people's opinions about me. God made you and me just the way he wanted us. Think about it: If we were all the same shade, height, weight, and shape the world would be a boring place to live. But thanks be to God that he has given us what I like to call the beauty of diversity. It's our diversity that makes us so unique. Your hair may not be like your friend's hair but it's your hair; your skin tone may not be like their skin tone but it's your skin tone; your voice may not be the pitch of someone else's voice but it's your voice. There's a passage of scripture in 1st Timothy 4:12 that reads "never let anyone think less of you; however, be the example in what you say, in how you live, in the way you love, your walk of faith, and pureness of heart."

One of our greatest assets is our diversity. I've learned how to stand firm in who I am and how God created me. When my wife and I celebrated the births of our two beautiful children, we were blessed with two babies of different shades of skin tone. My son shares my wife's Caramel Frappuccino complexion, while my daughter shares my deep Chocolate Espresso complexion. The reason I highlight this is because at the birth of my daughter I knew that skin tone would one day be a conversation. Knowing that this would one day be a conversation, I didn't want her complexion to be a complex to her. I began to educate myself so that I could educate my baby concerning the reason for her beautiful dark skin tone. Understand, many of our intimidations and inferiorities are due to a lack of information or the abundance of misinformation.

Just think about it for a moment: If you knew back then what you know now, you would not have run every time you were chased. You would not have cried every time someone hurt your feelings by saying something negative about you. You would not have cared when others who didn't know you, let alone know themselves, tried to make you feel as if you had no significance.

I discovered that education is the key to disarming the enemy of bigotry. I educated myself to know that the skin is the body's largest and heaviest organ. The skin's most obvious job is to protect the inside of the body from the environment, but there is much more to the skin than protection. Along with its role as a protective barrier, the skin helps us to maintain the right internal temperature. The skin allows us to sense the world through nerve endings. I shared with my chocolate princess that the skin has three basic layers: the epidermis, the dermis, and the hypodermis. The epidermis is the outermost layer. It is a waterproof barrier that gives skin its feel. The dermis serves as connective tissue and protects the body from stress and strain. It also gives the skin strength and elasticity. The hypodermis is the bottom layer of skin. Also known as subcutaneous tissue, the hypodermis insulates and protects the body, stores energy (fat), helps to regulate body temperature, and connects the skin to muscles and bones.

The most interesting part of educating my baby was this thing called melanin. Skin color is a phenotype, which is an observable trait like eye color or height. The color of our beautiful dark skin results from different types of a pigment called melanin. Melanin's primary role is to protect the skin from damaging ultraviolet light from the sun, which can cause skin cancer. When skin is exposed to ultraviolet light, melanocytes start producing melanin, creating a suntan. I told my baby girl not only is her dark skin pretty, it's also protective. Armed with this education, my chocolate princess has never felt inferior to anyone because of her melanin. I'm fully aware that bigotry and bias in the black community is an ongoing battle that we will overcome if we continue to love and educate ourselves on just how wonderfully God has created all of us.

All By Faith

You Shall Have Whatsoever You Say

> **Mark 11:22-24 (KJV)**
> *22 And Jesus answering saith unto them,*
> *Have faith in God.*
> *23 For verily I say unto you, That whosoever*
> *shall say unto this mountain, Be thou removed,*
> *and be thou cast into the sea; and shall not doubt*
> *in his heart, but shall believe that those things*
> *which he saith shall come to pass; he shall have*
> *whatsoever he saith.*
> *24 Therefore I say unto you, What things soever ye*
> *desire, when ye pray, believe that ye receive them,*
> *and ye shall have them.*

The power of prayer was instilled in my life at an early age. I can recall a typical school day would usually start with my mother saying, "Arise, shine, and give God the glory." It was at that very moment we would begin to hear a consistent combination of prayer, praise, and threats of peril if you didn't hurry to breakfast and make it out the door to catch the bus for school. Every morning before we departed for the day, my mother would pray and anoint my two brothers and me with so much oil that we would almost slip out of our clothes while sliding to catch the bus for school. It's no understatement to say that prayer was always a great part of our day. I can remember whispering a prayer against some of my irritable and unnecessary classmates, while sensing a strong need to intercede for the removal of some of the staff and teachers to faraway places. Often when we returned home from school, my mother could be heard in prayer, thanking God for keeping us all day. When we sat down to eat, we would take time to pray, giving thanks to God for food on the table, clothes on our backs, and shoes on our feet. Before going to bed Mama would spend time in prayer; she could be heard thanking God for His peace, His provisions, and His protection. Then Mama would ask God for something that made absolutely no sense to me at all. With tears running down and sincerity in Her Voice, Mama would say, "Lord, give me a praying spirit." I would be thinking, *A praying spirit—Mama, are you serious? You've been praying all day. Why don't you ask God for a new place to live, for a Cadillac, or just ask God to make me famous so that I can go on a date with Thelma Evans from Good Times?*

As a kid, I can recall prayer meetings were held in the homes of various members of our church aka the saints of God. We would gather in someone's home and call on the name of Jesus for what seemed to be hours on end. More often than not, my mother would volunteer our living room to be the meeting place for these weekly mid-day prayer gatherings. Can you imagine rushing home from school with an enthusiastic anticipation of watching your favorite after school program, only to find yourself in the middle of a prayer meeting? These prayer gatherings would be conducted by at least five women who were mad at the devil for being single, divorced, widowed, or sex deprived. It was with that passion and pent-up aggression that these women would do what we call pray heaven down. Being in the presence of these great prayer warriors is an experience that I will never forget. They would call on the name of Jesus and decree deliverance, healing, and miracles, all in the name of Jesus. I could feel the power of the Holy Ghost and knew that prayer had set the atmosphere for the manifested presence of God in that weekly mid-day prayer meeting. I truly believe that it was in those prayer meetings that God gave me this gift that I came to embrace called the Gift of Faith.

When I was in the fifth grade, I was blessed to have a teacher who went above the call of duty. Her name was Ms. Vanholten and she was a praying woman, to say the least. Ms. Vanholten had moved to the United States from Germany. One afternoon in class Ms. Vanholten was sharing her journey from Germany to the United States when she proclaimed that she moved to the U.S. all by faith. For some reason when Ms.Vanholten spoke those words all by faith it arrested my attention and I wanted to know more about this "all by faith." I can recall Ms. Vanholten, speaking with an accent that required you to listen closely not to miss anything that was being said, praying the blessings of the Lord over the class at the start and close of the day. There were times that I knew that God had sent Ms. Vanholten to speak directly to me. In addition to making sure that we received our lesson, Ms. Vanholten would pray in her soft German tone and make positive proclamations that have had an impact upon my life to this very day. It was this senior, seasoned woman from Germany who instilled in our fifth-grade class the importance of positive affirmations, private prayer, and that hugs heal. On one of our many days in class when all the students were seated with heads bowed, waiting for Ms. Vanholten to open in prayer, she did the unexpected. She asked me to stand and pray the blessing of the Lord upon our class. I stood up with no hesitation, and before I opened my mouth, Ms. Vanholten uttered these words to me: "YOU SHALL HAVE WHATSOEVER YOU SAY"—and then it happened. The Holy Spirit took over me and I began to utter God's praise and prophetic blessings over my fifth-grade class. When I took my seat, I knew without a doubt that I had no idea what just happened but I was sure that I wanted it to happen again.

It was the last day of school and Ms. Vanholten was standing at the entrance of our classroom. After her verbal congratulations for a great school year, Ms. Vanholten began gently resting her prayerful hands upon the heads of every child as they exited. I was the last one to exit, and while many of my classmates were excited about starting the summer, I knew that this would be the last day that I would enter and exit Ms. Vanholten's sanctuary of faith-filled affirmations, private prayers, and healing hugs, we called our fifth-grade classroom.

Overcome with emotions and not wanting to face the reality of the moment, I delayed as long as I could before leaving the sanctuary known as our fifth-grade classroom. All at once I walked swiftly through the doors that led to the start of the summer, not allowing Ms. Vanholten to take the time and rest her hand upon me as she normally would. Only five steps through the door, I turned to see this senior, seasoned woman from Germany, who instilled in our fifth-grade class the importance of faith-filled affirmations, private prayer, and healing hugs. There she stood with arms extended and heart open. I embraced this spirit-filled lady who had journeyed from Germany to the U.S all by faith, this noble woman who had taken the time to pray over me for the last nine months. As I hugged Ms. Vanholten, she began to speak in a language that spoke directly to God. At that very moment I knew with all certainty that this very special lady from so far away had been divinely sent to positively affirm, release private prayers, and give healing hugs. While releasing me from her embrace she spoke these words again, and again, and again" "You shall have whatsoever you say."

Before the days of the Internet, cell phones, iPod, Androids, or any social media Apple products, your sources of information were the morning paper, the six o'clock news, *Sports Illustrated,* and if you grew up in my neighborhood, *Ebony* and *Jet* magazines. However, our best source of information was the local barber shop.

When I was a kid Mr. Baker was our neighbor who lived across the street. He was also our back porch barber. Mr. Baker would come home from his day job with the city sanitation department and cut hair on his back porch until late in the evening. While getting your classic cut, you would be educated or debated on sports, politics, relationships, or religion. Sports talk was always about football on every level, from the Peewee league to the NFL. The topic of politics was usually about what the White House would be like if we ever elected a black president. Relationship conversations were the most enjoyable. I would learn so much just from listening to other people's experiences in dating, marriage, divorce, and just trying to make their relationships work.

Religion is and always will be a hot topic in the black barbershop. Every Saturday the barbershop would be standing room only. Fathers and sons could be seen waiting their turn to get into the barber's chair for that Sunday-go-to-church cut. Then it would happen; someone would say something like "I'm believing God by Faith" and the discussion would begin. Someone would ask, "So when you say that you're believing God by Faith, what does that really mean?" The response would sound something like this: "I'm decreeing and declaring that what I'm believing God for is going to happen for me and my family." My ears would be waiting to hear more and more. Mr. Baker would look at that brother who had taken center stage talking about decreeing and declaring by faith and say to them, "Say on, brother, say on." That brother would say with a conviction that was strong enough to move a mountain what he was believing for himself and his family. No one in the barber shop would say anything contrary. We would all begin to agree and affirm that what he said was going to happen for him and his family. Often it would be a declaration of a new job, a better place to live, an opportunity for the children's education, or a loved one getting well. Most everyone in the barber shop would start saluting each other with the words "you going to have what you say." Then it would happen: Someone would say that they were decreeing and declaring by faith that their favorite team was going to the Super Bowl and that's when the arguments would start.

I would walk home convinced that if I could just say it, then I would see it come to pass. I fell in love with this concept of "you shall have whatsoever you say." I believe that's where I fell in love with faith. Hear me when I tell you that I began saying things that would startle full-grown adults. My mind would be going faster than I could speak. My thoughts and beliefs became my agent of faith, while my words became my expression of faith. Ultimately my actions became my evidence of faith. To this very day I still stand firm and believe that what you think about will become your belief, and what you believe is what you'll say, and what you say, you'll act upon and accomplish. This has been the secret to my success. I really believe that all things are possible to those who believe that all things are possible. Call it crazy but think about how much more you could do if you just believed that you could do more. All this starts with a confession of faith. Your confession of faith is the key to your victory, your increase, and every one of your great accomplishments.

I believe that our confession of faith honors God and God honors our confession of faith. The Bible is clear in Hebrews 11:6 (KJV) that without faith it's impossible to please God. It is further emphasized in Romans 14:23 (KJV) that whatsoever is not of faith is sin. Sin, in one of my many personal opinions, is simply to be stuck in negativity. Therefore, whatsoever is not of faith is stuck in negativity.

We have an eternal God, therefore everything God has for us is birthed in eternity. The question is how, then, do I bring what God has for me in eternity into time? Here's the answer: by faith. Faith is God's eternal now; faith brings what God has in eternity into the now. The Bible says in Hebrews 11:1 (KJV), "Now faith is the substance of things hoped for, the evidence of things not seen." The confession of faith prospers our families, protects our families, and preserves our families. In Hebrews 11:20 (KJV), by faith Isaac blessed Jacob and Esau concerning things to come. Isaac blessed his two sons concerning things that had not yet happened.

The confession of faith has the power to reach into the future of the family and confirm what is to come. Just imagine what the next generation is going to be like because we are confirming by faith what is to come. At this present moment, my wife and I currently have no grandchildren; however, every night we confess that our grandchildren, our great-grandchildren, and our great-great-great grandchildren are blessed and not cursed. We confess this until I can see the faces of my precious grand-babies. It's this confession of your faith that's securing the future of your family. The Bible shows us in Hebrews 11:7 (KJV) that "by faith Noah, being warned of God of things not seen as of yet, moved with fear, prepared an ark to the saving of his house; by which he condemned the world, and became heir of the righteousness which is by faith." Noah was warned of God by faith of things not seen as yet. How many times has God given you a glimpse of the future for your family? Stop downplaying what God has revealed to you by faith and confess it. Noah was not only warned by faith of what was to come, Noah began to work toward it. Hebrews 11:7 says Noah moved with reverence and prepared an ark. Once you confess it, begin to prepare for it. This is exactly what Noah did; he moved on the revelation of the future by faith.

I came home one afternoon and told my wife that God had shown me a better home for our family. I then asked her to confess it with me. She confessed with me that night that God had a better home for us. We confessed it until she said, "Jason, I can see it by faith." The next afternoon when I returned home there were boxes packed at the door. I asked my wife what this was about and she said that she was working toward what had been revealed by faith.

Please understand we hadn't found a new home, we hadn't talked to a loan officer, we hadn't met with our real estate agent. We just confessed upon what God had warned us of and started preparing for it. Noah was warned, and Noah worked toward what he was warned about. Ultimately Noah won his family to God. It says in Hebrews 11:7 (KJV), "By faith Noah prepared an ark to the saving of his house." We moved into our new home not long after my wife started packing those boxes and just to think that it started with the confession of our faith. This move was a major win for our family at that time. I said to my wife one evening. "If it worked for Noah, it will work for us." What I was saying was if faith worked back then, faith will work now.

Always keep in mind it's your faith that's working. Never forget you and I were created to function in the likeness of God, and God created this whole universe with the confession of His mouth. The Bible says in Psalm 33:9 (KJV), "For he spake, and it was *done*; he commanded, and it stood fast." Just imagine, in the beginning the world was without form and void. Then God spoke and everything came to be. Genesis 1:3 says, "And God said, Let there be light: and there was light" (KJV). Things started to happen when God said, and things will happen when you say. I can recall as a child being told by my mother to do something and every time I would ask, "Why do I have to do this," she would respond, "Because I say so." It even got to a point that when I knew I was about to be asked to do something I would start moving in the direction that I needed to go to complete the assignment. That's just the kind of confidence that we should have in our confessions that we know and believe that whatever we confess is going to get completed. Job 22:28 (KJV) says, "Thou shalt also decree a thing, and it shall be established unto thee." It's your words that are changing your world. Your confession of faith is powerful enough to change your position in life and your conditions in life. I believe that your confession is powerful enough to birth every one of your desired possessions.

As we grow in our faith, we learn not to allow our current condition to alter our faith confession. There are times when God builds our faith in what I call the waiting rooms of life. The waiting room of life is when things don't happen as fast as we would like but we still commit to stand firm on our confession of faith. I encourage many who are confessing their faith, don't allow your situation to change your confession but allow your confession to change your situation. One of the better examples of confessing faith that I've ever heard was of a woman who had suffered with a flow of blood for twelve years. Just imagine having an issue that plagued you for twelve years. The difficulties this woman experienced are unimaginable. She went to physician after physician and didn't get any better, but her issue only kept getting worse. As if that wasn't bad enough, she had spent all her money in her endeavors to get better. However, despite her circumstances she had this determination that her condition would not be her conclusion. When she heard that Jesus was passing by she made a declaration of faith that would change her situation for the better. She declared, "If I can just touch a small piece of His clothing, I know that I will be made whole of this sickness." It was at that very moment things began to change. The Bible says in Mark 5:34 (KJV) that Jesus tuned to this woman and said, "Daughter, go in peace; thy faith hath made thee whole." Please note that this woman wasn't just healed; this woman was made whole. Her being made whole speaks of total restoration in every area of her life. This woman's faith in God restored everything that had been exhausted over the past twelve years. From the very moment she made her declaration of faith, in the words of my beloved sister, Dr. Patrina Steadman, there was "nothing missing, nothing lacking, and nothing broken." Let's go a little deeper and say it wasn't just her faith in God that got her healed and made whole. It was her Faith of God that transformed her life. While many may have faith in God, there are some who understand what it means to have the Faith of God. Mark 11:22 (KJV) says, "Have faith in God." You can't have the Faith of God until you have faith in God. Having faith in God is having faith in God's Person. It means having total faith in who God is. God has a way of allowing life to be a classroom to teach us just who He is. When there's a need you come to know God as Jehovah Jireh, the God who provides. When there's a sickness you learn that God is Jehovah Rapha, the Lord who heals. When things get crazy and chaotic, we learn that God is Jehovah Shalom, the Lord is Peace.

When the object of our faith becomes the person of God, we can then have faith in what God has promised. Having faith in God is having faith in what God has promised. It is knowing what God has said. There are many who like to convey what God is saying but have no clue what God said. I truly believe that to know what God is saying, you need to know what God has said. Know what God has promised to perform and have unshakable faith in every promise that He's made. I believe that our relationship with God is not a relationship of God just delivering us from all our problems but a relationship of God performing what he has promised. Truth: One of the reasons we face problems in life is to see God perform what He has promised. God will make promises in the areas of our lives that seem problematic. Consider Abraham and Sarah: God promised them a child knowing that they were old and Sarah was barren. However, God made the promise despite their age and emptiness. Abraham believed God in the face of the problems and received what God promised. That's what having faith in God does; it looks beyond the problem and sees the possibility of the promise. Having faith in God is also having faith in the power or the ability of God. This is what God meant when He asked in Genesis 18:14 (KJV), "Is there anything too hard for the Lord?" Sarah laughed at what God promised that He was going to do. I believe that Sarah's laugh was a laugh of disbelief in her ability to birth a child. At this point in life Sarah was beyond childbearing age and it has ceased to be with her after the manner of women. That's when God refocused her faith from her ability to His ability. In other words what God was saying was "never mind your ability, just have faith in my ability to perform what I promise to perform."

I'm sure that you can identify with me that there have been times you knew that if something was going to happen, it would have to be on God's ability. That new job with the corner office that you know you didn't qualify for—I know that was all God's ability. That family that was told that they couldn't get the approval for the new home because of several reasons and then the phone rang with great news—that was all God's ability. Getting accepted into that college on a full scholarship when you knew the truth about your grades—that was all God's ability. The offer to pastor that wonderful congregation with no formal training or experience was all on God's ability. I'm thankful that we can have faith in God's ability and not just our own. Having faith in God is also having faith in God's plan to perform what he has promised. This is where many lose focus and fall off the wagon. They have faith right up to the point of God's plan. Israel's exit from Egypt was not apart from God's plan. God told Moses that He was going to make it look like they were trapped in and had nowhere to go and Pharaoh was going to pursue after them. This looking defeated was all a part of the plan. However, when they arrived at the Red Sea and Pharaoh's army was behind them, Israel began to cry out to Moses in a panic. God allowed their panic to work into the plan. It was in their panic they were told to stand still and see what God would do for them that very day. This was all a part of God's divine plan.

I've learned, for every area of our lives God has a plan, and God's plans are without fail. Having faith in God is having faith in God's plans. When it comes to our destiny, Jeremiah 29:11 (KJV) reveals God's plan. When it comes to our deficit, John 6:5,6 (KJV) reveals God's plan. When it comes to our dividends, Proverbs 3:9,10 (KJV) reveals God's plan. When it comes to our deliverance, Exodus 14 (KJV) reveals God's plan. Having faith in the plans of God opens the doors for the opportunity to speak by faith, believe by faith, and receive by faith. Mark 11:23 (KJV) says, "For verily I say unto you, That whosoever shall say unto this mountain, Be thou removed, and be thou cast into the sea; and shall not doubt in his heart, but shall believe that those things which he saith shall come to pass; he shall have whatsoever he saith." Having the faith of God is speaking, believing, and receiving what we decree by faith. Having the faith of God is speaking to the impossibilities. Having the faith of God is believing what you say shall come to pass. Having the faith of God is receiving what you say.

Faith to Forgive

Giving Yourself Permission to Move On

> ### Luke 17:3-5 (KJV)
> *³ Take heed to yourselves: If thy brother trespass against thee, rebuke him; and if he repent, forgive him.*
> *⁴ And if he trespass against thee seven times in a day, and seven times in a day turn again to thee, saying, I repent; thou shalt forgive him.*
> *⁵ And the apostles said unto the Lord, Increase our faith.*

Although God graces us with this great opportunity to speak, believe, and receive, we must be aware of one of the greatest oppositions and obstructions that we will ever face in having the faith of God fully and effectively. This dreadful opposition and obstruction is unforgiveness.

Your faith in God is futile if there's any unforgiveness. Many have asked me about the obstruction of unbelief and uncertainty, but I know firsthand the greatest enemy of faith is unforgiveness. Mark 11:25-26 (KJV) says, "And when ye stand praying, forgive, if ye have ought against any: that your Father also which is in heaven may forgive you your trespasses. But if ye do not forgive, neither will your Father which is in heaven forgive your trespasses." The faith of God is the ability to speak, believe, and receive total forgiveness. Forgiveness is the permission that you give yourself to move on.

That's right: Give yourself permission to move on. Letting go of past hurts and pains releases us into the future ahead. Forgiveness must be deliberate and intentional. The intent behind forgiveness must be love for oneself. Self-love is what so many are lacking. We spend so much time loving others that we neglect to love ourselves. When we do show love to ourselves it's oftentime at the spa or shopping for something nice. All those things are well and good, but I believe the most powerful gift you can give yourself is the gift of forgiveness. This permission to move on is so necessary to live and enjoy the life that God has given to us.

Jesus came to the earth to fulfill an assignment, and this assignment was to be our earthly example of how to forgive. Throughout scripture there are many examples of people who forgave and moved on to experience greater things. One of the primary things that God expects us to do as believers is to forgive. Let's be honest—this is easier said than done. This power of forgiveness is evident in those who choose to forgive and give themselves permission to move on. When we forgive others, we are freeing ourselves from the bondage, power, and stronghold that the enemy has over us and releasing ourselves to a greater future. The Bible tells us that God expects us to forgive as many times as we need to. In other words, give yourself as much permission to release the hurts of the past as you need. Peter asked Jesus in Matthew 18:21, 22 (KJV) how often or how many times he should forgive those who had offended him. "No, not seven times," Jesus replied, "but seventy times seven!" This proves to us that there is no limitation to how many times we need to forgive others and give ourselves permission to move on.

One of my favorite forgiveness stories in the Bible is about a young man named Joseph. One day Joseph told his brothers about two dreams he had. His brothers hated him because of his dreams. They concluded that Joseph was telling them that he would rule over them. Joseph's parents didn't appreciate what the dreams were conveying to them either. Because of Joseph's dreams his brothers devised a plot to kill him. They eventually decided to sell him to some merchants, headed down to Egypt, and told his father that he was killed by some wild animal. It was there in Egypt that Joseph ended up as a slave under Potiphar. And just when it seemed as if things couldn't get any worse, Potiphar had Joseph thrown into prison because of Mrs. Potiphar's false allegations of rape. God eventually elevated Joseph to become second in command to Pharaoh. Many years later

Joseph met his brothers when they came to Egypt looking for food during the time of a severe famine that would last seven years. Upon their arrival Joseph recognized his brothers, but they did not recognize him. It wasn't until he revealed to them that he was their brother that they knew who he was. Ultimately, Joseph was reconciled with his brothers and did not hold any resentment against them. He embraced them and told them that God had sent him ahead of them to preserve their lives. I believe that Joseph's heart had come to forgive his brothers before he ever saw them again. It was the faith to forgive that gave Joseph the permission to move on and become greater.

Jesus gave a parable in the gospel of Luke, chapter 15. This parable tells of a man who had two sons. The younger son desired of his father his share of the inheritance and the father willingly gave it to him. Not long after, the son departed into a faraway place and squandered his wealth in wild living. A famine came on the land and the young man found himself destitute after he blew his inheritance. He could not afford to eat, and he got a job as a farmhand, charged with feeding pigs. The only food available to him was that which the pigs ate. At that point, he decided to go back home and ask his father if he could be like one of the servants. I believe most fathers would have rebuked their sons for making such foolish decisions. However, the father instead received his son with open arms. This father reinstated his son by giving him a ring, a coat, and shoes. The father went on to rejoice by throwing a party in his son's honor—pretty awesome when you consider what his son did. I personally love the part of the parable when the father sees his son from afar and runs to meet him. That's an open display of the love that covers and forgives a multitude of sins. 1st Peter 4:8 (KJV): "And above all things have fervent charity among yourselves: for charity shall cover the multitude of sins." It is not possible for a relationship to be reconciled without those involved forgiving each other and a willingness to accept each other back into each other's life. What we learn from the father in this parable is forgiveness opens the door for reconciliation of relationships. Forgiveness releases us from the hurt that has kept us tied to the past. Forgiveness gives us permission to move on, and forgiveness is a great part of having the Faith of God. I know forgiveness can be a difficult thing for many.

Let's consider Stephen's great example in the book of Acts. Stephen was a godly man who preached the gospel fearlessly. Some who did not want to hear the good news of Jesus Christ falsely accused him, and he was taken to the council to give an answer to the charges against him. Those who were not happy about what Stephen was doing dragged him out of the city and stoned him to death. Right before Stephen died, he looked up to heaven and saw Jesus standing at the right hand of God. He knelt and with a loud voice said, in Acts 7: 60 (KJV), "Lord, do not hold this sin against them." When he had said this, he died. While in the midst of being killed, Stephen forgave those who stoned him to death. He did not hold a grudge against them because he knew that God's will was for him to forgive them. He could have cursed them; he could have asked God to judge them for this harsh treatment, but he didn't. He forgave and gave himself permission to move on. Stephen displayed a depth of faith that allowed him to be concerned for those who were killing him. Stephen prayed that God wouldn't hold this action against them. Stephen reveals to us that it's possible to forgive others even when they are not regretful or remorseful for what they have done or are doing to you. Know that not all who offend you will bother to ask for your forgiveness, and we cannot afford to wait for them to do so. We are to forgive everyone and give ourselves permission to move on.

I conclude this chapter with Jesus, our greatest example of forgiveness. Jesus' life teaches us the importance and power of forgiveness. Jesus also had to forgive those who mistreated him and those who crucified Him. While on the cross, Jesus said, in Luke 23:34 (KJV), "Father, forgive them, for they do not know what they do." By saying this, He was choosing not to hold anything against those who crucified Him. This is the same thing we see in Stephen's story in the book of Acts, chapter seven. Jesus had twelve chosen disciples, and Judas was the disciple who betrayed Him with a kiss. Judas was considered a close friend of Jesus. After all, Judas ate with Jesus daily. Judas walked and talked with Jesus regularly. Judas saw Jesus perform miracles and experienced the pureness of Jesus' love. Yet Judas chose thirty pieces of silver over Jesus, his friend. Although Judas experienced remorse, He didn't repent and ask for forgiveness. Feeling bad for what you did is not the same as repentance and forgiveness. Despite this, Jesus harbored no anger, resentment, or bitterness toward Judas. Those close to us can hurt us, and we must be willing to forgive them. Truthfully, the offense usually hurts more when it is those who are close to us.

David said in Psalm 41:9 (KJV), "Yea, mine own familiar friend, in whom I trusted, which did eat of my bread, hath lifted up *his* heel against me." Although in verse 10 of this Psalm, David is asking God for the strength to repay them for what they did to Him, let's just focus on the forgiveness that Jesus displays. From Jesus, we learn that we should forgive even our close friends who offend us, in order to keep our hearts right and not fall into bitterness, and ultimately give yourself the permission to move on.

Overcoming the Fear of Failure

He Got My Book Out of the Trash

I've been very open and transparent about some of my upbringing, and it's no secret that I didn't graduate high school. At one time in my life, I was very embarrassed about the fact that I didn't get my high school diploma. Because of this embarrassment I would often withdraw from many conversations and remove myself from certain surroundings, all because of my failure to acquire my high school diploma. Perhaps you can identify with me, because I really believe that all of us have some area in our lives where we have felt embarrassed because of something that we did not obtain or something that we did not do that constantly makes us feel less than inadequate, insufficient, and downright unsatisfactory.

By the grace of God, I have arrived at a point in life where I'm confident and not afraid to face the giants and deal with the reasons and realities of my failed pursuit of my diploma. I was sixteen when I made a decision that would change the remainder of my teenage years. With a multitude of personal distractions and family problems, I decided that getting my GED would be the best thing for me to advance myself in life. In all honesty, I had no idea that going after my GED would prove to be more difficult than I could have ever imagined. When I received my study manual it literally looked like a 1980s Yellow Page phone book. I was determined, my mind was made up, and I had set my heart on getting my general education diploma. Obtaining a high school diploma may not seem like a major thing to you; however, in our house going to college was not something that was often discussed. Most people we knew were satisfied with receiving a high school diploma, although those who didn't graduate high school were frowned upon. I can remember hearing the conversations of ladies talking about the men that other women were interested in or dating. They would say things like "did he finish high school?" Or "where did he attend high school and what year did he graduate? Do you know anyone from his graduating class?" The moment they would name the high school and the year that he graduated and perhaps someone who could confirm his diploma, it was an automatic stamp of approval.

I would hear my parents and school personnel say things like without a high school diploma you'll never be able to get a good job. They would say the trash man needs a diploma, the mailman needs a diploma, the bus driver needs a diploma. None of these occupations interested me at all; however, I got the message. It was stamped in my mind that to do well in life I would need my high school diploma. My journey toward obtaining my general education diploma would take me from sunny South Florida to Washington, DC to Philadelphia Pennsylvania to Northern Virginia. South Florida was where I started the pursuit of my general education diploma. Philadelphia, Pennsylvania is where I continued my pursuit to obtain my general education diploma. Washington, DC is where I was tutored for my general education diploma and Northern Virginia is where I finally obtained my general education diploma. Trust me when I say that it sounds a lot easier than it was.

The reason I wrote this chapter was to encourage somebody to start and continue and finish your pursuit. I must be totally honest; I did not obtain my general education diploma on my own faith. I had to use someone else's faith to finish. I took morning, afternoon, and evening classes to prepare for the general education exam. This proved to be a tedious task, but I was determined. After 12 weeks of studying, I knew that I was ready. I went to bed late and woke up early night after night. Studying all night throughout the day, lunch breaks, on the subway, and the bus ride home, I was really determined to pass this test. I took the practice exam, and my instructor told me that she was sure that I would do well. I was scheduled to arrive by 7am to be in place for the exam that would start promptly at 7:30am. The night before my exam I went to bed early to ensure that I was properly rested and ready. I could feel that obtaining my general education diploma would change my life for the better. I could only envision how proud my parents would be of me, how I would be able to hold my head up and participate in conversations and not feel embarrassed or ashamed about not finishing high school.

The exam lasted three hours. Can you imagine cramming 12 years of school into a three-hour test? I was ready not only to receive my general education diploma; I was ready for this weight of embarrassment and feelings of inadequacy, insufficiency, and downright dissatisfaction to be lifted. I was ready to hold my head up and to feel like I had accomplished something worth being proud of. I know it's not a Bachelor's, Master's, or Ph.D. However, this was my GED. I was fully aware that there would be no GED class reunion, there would be no GED class pictures, there would be no annual GED celebration of accomplishment among classmates. After I completed my exam, sealed my test and exited the classroom, I knew that I had done my best. It took about two weeks to receive the results in the mail. Every day you could find me checking the mailbox anxiously awaiting the arrival of my test results.

One afternoon my younger brother Justin had gotten home and beat me to the mailbox. He came running upstairs with this big smile on his face and excitement in his voice. "Jason," he said, "I have your test results; open them up," he began to shout. I took a deep breath and opened that envelope, only to realize that I had failed by two points. I couldn't believe it—for two whole weeks I waited, only to find out that I had failed. I looked at my brother in utter disbelief and shook my head. I was disappointed, to say the least. I couldn't believe that I didn't pass. Justin looked at me and said, "Take the test again."

I was just two points away so there was no doubt in my mind that I wasn't going to retake the exam. I hurried to reschedule my test. I was told that I could retake the exam in thirty days. The thirty days gave me more time to study and gave me more time to prepare; after all, I only missed it by two points.

My thirty days had come to an end, and I was ready to move forward. I felt better prepared for my second attempt than I was at my first to pass the exam. Once again, I showed up at 7am, ready to have this weight lifted and this embarrassment removed, along with these feelings of inadequacy, insufficiency, and downright dissatisfaction. Because this was my second time testing, I was more familiar with the process. Honestly, I was more confident this time. I said my pretest prayer, knowing that this would be the day that my life would be changed forever.

To my surprise, when I opened my exam packet, this was not the same test that I had taken before. I immediately went to the exam instructor to address this catastrophe. I was met with the revelation that everyone has a different test. At that very moment I was gripped by the fear that

I would fail. In my mind I could hear the ongoing judgment of people I didn't even know. I saw myself defeated and depleted. I felt that I couldn't pass, let alone complete, this exam. The fear of failure had paralyzed me mentally, emotionally, and spiritually. I didn't want to try because I knew that I would fail. In all honesty, I never accepted that I failed the first time. I looked at it as if I just missed passing by two points. That's exactly what I would tell anyone who would ask how I did on the test. I would say with an air of confidence that I just missed it by two points; however, when I was alone this fear of failure seemed to be my constant reality. I just sat there and looked around for a few moments and decided that this wasn't for me anymore. After I completed a few questions on the test with little effort and no faith toward passing, I got up from my seat, placed my test in the exam box, and walked out without saying a word.

When I got home that evening Justin asked me, "How do you think you did?"

I responded, "It wasn't the same test." Justin said, "Ok what does that mean?" I said, "Justin, when I saw that it was a different test, I became even more afraid that I wouldn't pass." Justin asked, "So what did you do?" "I went through the motions of filling in a few of the questions with little to no effort."

After explaining what happened, I took a general education study manual to the trash incinerator and resolved that getting my general education diploma just wasn't for me. I tossed my books and study guide into the trash with the hopes of never seeing them again. I allowed this fear of failure and frustration to cancel out what I had believed in and worked so hard for. It is said that fear kills more dreams than failure ever will. In all honesty, we are guaranteed to miss every shot we don't take. Over ninety percent of people who fail are not actually defeated. Most simply quit and give up and refuse to go on.

I was told by a very wise man, "Don't fear failure but fear being in the exact same place next year as you are today." Those words shook me to the core; just to imagine being in the same place the following year was not an option. I decided that I would face my fears and overcome failure at any cost. Many would define failure as you didn't succeed. I've learned that failure by God's definition is that you didn't try. I'm reminded of the story in the Bible recorded in Matthew chapter 25 about the man who buried his talent because he was afraid he would fail. This man didn't even try. The story goes on to say that because of his fear of failure, what he had was taken and given to someone who wasn't afraid to try. I had to resolve that even if I didn't pass the general education diploma test, I could no longer be afraid to try.

Well, I wasn't the only one who was determined to see me win. My younger brother Justin decided that my pursuit of my general education diploma wasn't over. He went down to the basement of the apartment building, got into the dumpster and found my study manual. I'm grateful because Justin has always believed in me, perhaps more than I believed in myself. When I was a young amateur boxer, Justin believed in me to the point he would carry my gym bag to and from workouts. When I was a musician Justin believed in me to the point he would suggest that I enter the school talent shows, and I even won a few times. Even now that I am a minster of the gospel Justin believes in me so that he often drives three hours one way just to come hear me preach. What a great feeling to have someone believe in you despite the opposition and regardless of the outcome.

By the time I got back home there was a smell in the apartment that was beyond words. I asked Justin about the smell, and he replied, "It's your study manual. After you left, I went down to the dumpster and found it." He went on to say, "Jason, I know you can pass this test if you just keep trying." He said, "Remember, it's not how many times you fail that counts; it's how you feel when you succeed."

Again, I prepared myself to take the exam, showing up at 7am just as I did before. The only difference was the weight of embarrassment and feelings of inadequacy, insufficiency, and downright dissatisfaction didn't matter anymore. Those were all the things feeding my fear of failure. I knew I could pass the test, but I had to do it without the fear of failure overshadowing my thoughts. I said my prayers and began. This also was a completely different test than before, but I handled it like a boss. When I finished the last question, I sighed in relief and said to myself, *The fear of failure will never plague me ever again.* Of course, I wanted to pass but more than that, I knew that I wouldn't be in the same place that I was the year before. The fear that had paralyzed me and kept me in the same place for so many years was broken. A few weeks later I received my test results, and in all honesty, I wasn't surprised that I had passed. I was more grateful that I failed, because had it not been for my failure, I would not have faced this fear of failure. My prayer is that you're never afraid to fail, but fear being in the same place you're in this time next year.

Fatherhood

Fully Able to Handle Every Responsibility

Believe it or not, the thought of being a father has been in my mind since I was a child. Crazy as it may seem, as a kid I would visualize myself driving down the street with my superstar wife Thelma Evans from the 70s sitcom *Good Times*. However, my vision of Thelma and me had nothing to do with living in the Chicago projects. We would be in our conversion van with all my children. James, Florida, Michael, and J.J. were so happy for us, because in my imagination, we had already experienced different strokes and were moving on up to the east side. That's right, to a deluxe apartment in the sky. As a kid envisioning fatherhood, this would have been the facts of life.

I laugh when I think about me and Thelma in a conversion van full of kids. Thank God we don't stay in the imagination stage of life. By the time I was 24 God had graced me to meet an amazing young lady named Sonja that I asked to be my wife. Sonja and I have been married for almost 30 years. I'm sure my wife will agree with me that one of the greatest joys of our marriage has been raising our two children. I have said to some of my close friends that fatherhood was a gift that God granted me.

I was 27 when our first child was born, happy and elated that God had graced us with a healthy child, David Jarrel (DJ). David was born September 23, 2000. That's a day I will never forget. When David was being birthed into the world, to our surprise there was this silence that put a look of great concern on the faces of the doctor's delivery team. There wasn't the normal cry from an infant that indicated a sign of life from a child entering the world. There was a silence that caused a cry from my belly. In that delivery room I cried out the name of Jesus so loud until David cried back. The doctor looked at me with tear-filled eyes and said, "That did it; that did it!"

I learned from that day forward that it was my responsibility as a father to cry on behalf of my children. The truth is, fatherhood has taught me how to constantly cry on behalf of my children. The day my wife and I were given the news that we would be giving birth to a daughter, I literally cried. I cried because I knew that it would take every fiber of my being to protect my baby girl from everything that wasn't likened to God. It was the summer of 2003, August 25th, to be exact, that Jasmine (Jazzy) was born. That was the day my life again changed forever.

One day while holding David and Jasmine in my arms, I asked my wife how she thought that I was doing as a father. She responded, "Jason, you were a father long before we ever had children." She went on to tell me that she didn't marry me just because she was madly in love with her best friend. She expressed that she saw the potential of a great father. I thought to myself, *I'm glad she didn't see me and Thelma Evans in that conversion van with all of those children.* My wife went on to express how important it is for women to marry a man not just because they think he would make a good husband but to marry someone that has the potential of being a great father. We began to have this discussion that all husbands don't make good fathers, but good fathers make great husbands. Don't get me wrong; being a good husband is very important. The word husband comes from two words: house and band. Therefore, the husband is the band that holds the house together. So, it's vitally important to be a great husband. The truth is, not every man will become a husband. Some have decided that singleness is what's best for them, and I get it. However, I believe that the mandate has been placed on every man to be a father. To define what a father is I use this acronym: Fully Able to Handle Every Responsibility. From this definition it is clear to see there's a great mandate for men to become fathers.

Our land has been struck with a curse. In the last half of the previous century, we have seen an incredible increase in crime, violence, drugs and gangs—and although legislators and economists offer various solutions, the real root of the problem is negligent fathers and unparented children.

In the past, fathers have failed our society. They have abandoned the home and left mothers to raise children by themselves. The ones who have stayed at home have often neglected the most important duty of fathers, and that is to be the priests in the home. The good news is God has promised a revival of fatherhood in the last days. I've come to understand that most men know very little about what makes a good father. And many women would choose a man who's fit to be a husband rather than a man who understands the mandate of being a father. Just because he's a baby daddy doesn't mean that he's a father. I said to someone that having children doesn't make you a father any more than standing in your garage makes you a car.

As a result of not knowing what it means to be a father, we often make the attempt and strive to give our children everything that we didn't have. I've seen this more times than I care to recall, where a man feels that to be a great father, he has to give his children everything that they desire. Often when we are doing this it's because we are trying to make up for a lack in our own childhood or something that we failed to do. There are those whose motivation for fatherhood is fueled by the competition of his father of his upbringing. This not only happens with men but women as well. The competitive parenting method is not wise. Constantly competing with your past is not the pathway to being a great father. I used to say things like when I have children, I will never allow my kids to go through whatever negativity that I was experiencing at the hands of my father. I'm not suggesting that we shouldn't strive to give the next generation a better life, nor am I implying that our fathers were not the best. I would never do that, not at all.

If you would allow me to take a point from a personal perspective, my dad was very much present in my life. From my earliest childhood I can remember my dad being there to support my brothers and me in whatever we were interested in doing. I believe that my dad did the best he could with what he had. He would give his last and go the extra mile. My dad was like the neighborhood dad to many of my friends. Growing up in the projects, many of the kids didn't know who their dads were. Some had never seen their fathers, and many were left with broken promises from a man who never showed up.

I was having lunch a few weeks ago with some colleagues when the topic of conversation shifted to marriage and parenting. I was shocked to hear one of the men with whom I was meeting with say that he had never met his father before. Everyone in this meeting is above forty years of age and this man said he has never met his dad. I trust that it didn't show on my face, but I was stunned to hear this from someone who has children of his own and in my opinion is a great father to his own sons. I took the liberty and began to ask what that feels like and what effect it has had on his life to this point. He responded, "I've struggled through many relationships, and find it very difficult to deal with senior men who could possibly be in the age range of my unknown dad." He went on to say that most of the women he's dated didn't have fathers in their lives, or father figures. I asked, "Do you think that could be an issue with relationships not working?" He looked at me, paused, sighed and said, "You know, I've never thought about it." We further discussed that every man has the mandate of fatherhood on his life and to be involved with a woman who didn't have a father or father figure can be challenging.

I am sure that there are some who may not agree with me on this, but I'm not writing this for your approval or applause. I'm writing this to help someone who may be struggling with the absence of fatherhood. It's no secret the world has discounted the importance of fathers, yet the biblical definition of a family is fatherhood. Ephesians 3:14-15 (KJV): "For this cause I bow my knees unto the Father of our Lord Jesus Christ, of whom the whole family in heaven and earth is named." The Greek word "family" is patria, and it is derived from the root pater. For those who know either Greek or Latin, you recognize that this word means "father." To define a family in the biblical sense, therefore, is to call it "fatherhood." Without a father, there is no family. The proof of this is that the family gets their name from the father. The biblical definition of an orphan is to be "fatherless." It's not to be without both parents, but to simply be without a father, and so we have a whole flock of children in our land who are orphans. Without fathers the family cannot grow to become all God intended for it. The father is the root of the family, and if the root is bad, the family will likely have trouble. Isaiah 1:5 (KJV): "Why should ye be stricken anymore? ye will revolt more and more: the whole head is sick, and the whole heart faint."

My wife and I have been married almost thirty years and I know that when we stood at the altar and exchanged vows, the reason she took my last name was because I became her father. Hence why they ask in the wedding ceremony who gives this woman to marry. It's normally her father or a father figure that gives her to marry. She goes from one father to another; she is never without fatherhood. She transfers from one fully able to handle every responsibility to another fully able to handle every responsibility. God's definition of Family is Fatherhood. Ephesians 3:14-15 (KJV): "For this cause I bow my knees unto the Father of our Lord Jesus Christ, Of whom the whole family in heaven and earth is named." I believe if we took this more seriously, women wouldn't be so quick to desire a husband and not a father. The honor and respect that a wife gives to her husband starts with the honor and respect she gives her father. If she has never given honor or respect to her father or a father figure, then how can she be expected to honor the father in her husband? I hear men say this often about women that they don't get along with: "She is disrespectful." Why does he feel so disrespected? Because more often than not, he may be dealing with a woman who has never had respect and honor for her father or a father figure.

When a man doesn't have respect for his father or a father figure, it can be very difficult for him to love any woman like Christ loves the church. The saving love that Christ displays for the church is in direct connection with pleasing His father. When we first come to know God, we don't know Him as our Lord and savior. We know him first as our everlasting father, according to Isaiah 9:6 (KJV): "…The mighty God, The everlasting Father, The Prince of Peace." Christ doesn't become our savior until the gospel of Matthew 1:21 (KJV): "And she shall bring forth a son, and thou shalt call his name JESUS: for he shall save his people from their sins." Always remember God is father first. This is how we have been instructed to pray. Matthew 6:9 (KJV): "After this manner therefore pray ye: Our Father which art in heaven, Hallowed be thy name." This is the divine order from God our heavenly father. As it is in heaven, so it is in the earth. God compares nothing to His church but marriage. The order of the marriage is the man must be father first.

This goes for our relationships with our children as well as spouses. As much as I love my son and daughter, and God knows that I would do anything for them, this must be understood before I'm anything to them or do anything for them. They first know me as father, the one who is fully able to handle every responsibility. A great part of the preparation for the manifestation of our savior was turning hearts of fathers to their children. Malachi 4:5-6

(KJV): "Behold, I will send you Elijah the prophet before the coming of the great and dreadful day of the LORD: And he shall turn the heart of the fathers to the children, and the heart of the children to their fathers." In preparation for the coming of Christ, the prophet was to turn the hearts of the father to the children and turn the hearts of the children to the fathers. I believe that God is still turning hearts to the father. In the Garden of Eden, the first Adam turned from the father and birthed sin in the land. In the garden of Gethsemane, the last Adam turned to the father and brought salvation to all people.

One of the most profound illustrations of a father-son relationship in the Bible is the story of Abraham and Isaac. In Genesis 17:5 (KJV) Abraham's name is changed from Abram to Abraham. This name means father of many nations. Although at that time Abraham didn't have any children, God knew that there was a mandate of fatherhood on his life. The Bible says that God chose Abraham because he knew that he would be a great example to his family. Genesis 18:19 (KJV): "For I know him, that he will command his children and his household after him, and they shall keep the way of the LORD, to do justice and judgment; that the LORD may bring upon Abraham that which he hath spoken of him." In Romans 4:16 (KJV) Abraham is called the father of us all: "but to that also which is of the faith of Abraham; who is the father of us all." In this story recorded in Genesis chapter 22 God calls Abraham to offer his only son Isaac as an offering. Abraham, out of faith, trust, and obedience, takes his son Isaac to the place

God has shown him in the distance. What is seen in this story is what every father should strive to give his family. Genesis 22:7-8 (KJV): "And Isaac spake unto Abraham his father, and said, My father: and he said, Here *am* I, my son. And he said, Behold the fire and the wood: but where *is* the lamb for a burnt offering? And Abraham said, My son, God will provide himself a lamb for a burnt offering: so they went both of them together." What Abraham the father of Isaac provides is what our heavenly father provides when we turn to Him. Isaac has a concern, and his father provides him with a level of comfort that keeps him going.

I declare that every concern that you will ever have will be met with the Father's comfort. As a father let's put ourselves in Abraham's shoes—how do you think Abraham felt as he led his only son up to that place of sacrifice? Every father knows the dangers and disappointments of the world that we live in, and yet we take full comfort in the fact that God is in control. As fathers we must seek God for the proper words to use when we need to comfort our children. It's those words of comfort that assure us that God will provide. As Abraham and Isaac continued, they came to the place that God had told Abraham of, and there Abraham built an altar. The altar is the place of sanctification, sacrifice, and service. It was at this altar that Abraham demonstrated his confidence in God. Genesis 22:9-10 (KJV): "And they came to the place which God had told him of; and Abraham built an altar there, and laid the wood in order, and bound Isaac his son, and laid him on the altar upon the wood. And Abraham stretched forth his hand and took the knife to slay his son." I believe wholeheartedly that Isaac did not know what was planned for him. Although Abraham knew, as a father Abraham put total faith in God that everything was going to be all right. During all of this Isaac sees the confidence of his father and remains calm as he assists his father in building an altar in preparation for his death. If we as fathers cannot maintain a true confidence in God and live it out daily before our families, how can we expect our children to maintain a confidence in us?

The next thing we see in the story is that Abraham exemplifies an uncompromising commitment. Commitment is important to any relationship, especially the relationships between a father and his children. It is said that success on any level is not just because of talent and ability but the majority that succeed do so because of an unwavering commitment. Please understand there is a vast difference between interest and commitment. While many may be interested, not all are committed. When you're interested in doing something, you do it only when it's convenient. When you're committed to something, you accept the challenge and take no excuses. As fathers, without commitment, we will experience very little to no lasting success. Fatherhood is all about commitment. This means staying loyal to what you said you were going to do long after the sensation you said it in has departed.

I got a call from my wife one day that my daughter Jazzy had achieved something notable in school. Jazzy was so excited about her great accomplishment that she couldn't wait to tell all about it. In my excitement for her, I promised that I would take her to Sweet Frog, a local ice cream shop, for her favorite flavor with all the toppings. Five hours later, I arrived home tired as a Hebrew slave. As I open the door my baby girl was singing and dancing throughout the house that her daddy was taking her to Sweet Frog. My wife could see the look of exhaustion on my face and was about to offer an alternate suggestion. Just then I thought about my commitment beyond the sensation of the moment and gathered myself and took my baby girl to Sweet Frog. Believe it or not, Jazzy has no recollection of her classroom great achievement, but she does remember me keeping my commitment and taking our ride to Sweet Frog.

It was the commitment of Abraham that led to the second call. The first call was a call to sacrifice the substitute ram in the bush. Genesis 22:11-13 (KJV): "And the angel of the LORD called unto him out of heaven, and said, Abraham, Abraham: and he said, Here *am* I. And he said, Lay not thine hand upon the lad, neither do thou anything unto him: for now I know that thou fearest God, seeing thou hast not withheld thy son, thine only *son* from me. And Abraham lifted up his eyes, and looked, and behold behind *him* a ram caught in a thicket by his horns: and Abraham went and took the ram and offered him up for a burnt offering in the stead of his son." God intervened in this situation just in time, telling Abraham that a ram had been provided in place of his son Isaac. The second call is the call of compound blessings. A father's commitment will always lead to the second call. It's the joy of every father to hear the second call. The second call changed everything in the life of Abraham. This was the call that made everything worth it. The second call is the call of divine approval. This should be the goal of every father—to hear the approval of our heavenly father. Genesis 22:15-18 (KJV): "And the angel of the LORD called unto Abraham out of heaven the second time, And said, By myself have I sworn, saith the LORD, for because thou hast done this thing, and hast not withheld thy son, thine only *son*: That in blessing I will bless thee, and in multiplying I will multiply thy seed as the stars of the heaven, and as the sand which *is* upon the sea shore; and thy seed shall possess the gate of his enemies; And in thy seed shall all the nations of the earth be blessed; because thou hast obeyed my voice."

Every father wants to feel that he's gotten it right. Fatherhood isn't an easy assignment, but it is very rewarding. As fathers we will make mistakes and bad decisions. The scriptures reveal that Abraham made his fair share of both mistakes and bad decisions. However, God kept His commitment with Abraham. That must be the goal of every father: to keep our commitment. If we, through the grace of God, strive to keep our commitment, it will lead to the second call.

Oh, what joy, to hear the sound of the second call. The call that opens our eyes to see beyond the barriers of life and live beyond the limitations. What joy awaits everyone who sees the greater that lies beyond the tests of life. Whether they be tests of walking into what you believe, or refusing to go back to what you came out of, or standing firm and decreeing that every snare of the enemy is broken. Stand in the liberty that God has graced you to overcome every fear and see the greater by faith. God said that He will never leave or fail you. Go forward knowing that He's always there to love you, lead you, and lift you to see greater.

www.ingramcontent.com/pod-product-compliance
Lightning Source LLC
Chambersburg PA
CBHW070133100426
42744CB00009B/1822